D1234297

ONLY AS ONE

THE WORDS AND WISDOM
OF
REX DOCKERY

by
Wallene T. Dockery

EDITED BY
BOB PHILLIPS

ILLUSTRATED BY
TED WATTS

SPORTS MARKETING, INC.

PUBLISHERS DATA

Design and selection ©1985 Sports Marketing, Inc.
Compilation of quotations and illustrations ©S.M.I.

First Edition

Second Printing 1985

Library of Congress Catalog number 85-63031.

Shared Publishing with Elkington & Keltner, GSA Corporation, and Fogelman Properties.

Published by ©S.M.I. in the United States of America, 1985.

ISBN 0-936169-00-1

TABLE OF CONTENTS

DEDICATION

In memory of Chris Faros, Charles Greenhill,
Glenn Jones, and Rex Dockery.

"To every thing there is a season."

—Ecclesiastes 3:1

LARRY COYNE, MEMPHIS PRESS-SCIMITAR

ONLY AS ONE

Now this is the law of the jungle
As old and as true as the sky,
And the wolf that shall keep it will prosper,
But the wolf that shall break it must die.

As the vine that girdles the tree trunk,
The law runneth forward and back.
The strength of the pack is the wolf
And the strength of the wolf is the pack.

And this is the law of athletics,
As true as the flight of the ball,
And the player that keeps it shall prosper,
But the player that breaks it must fall.

As the ball and parts that it's made of
Are bound and held fast with the seam,
The strength of the team is the player,
The strength of the player, the team.

— Author Unknown

INTRODUCTION

"Successful teams are a family of one," Rex Dockery often told his players. "There is strength in numbers. It's called teamwork and togetherness."

On December 12, 1983 — just one week after being named Metro Conference Coach of the Year — the Memphis State head football coach boarded a small plane with an assistant coach, Chris Faros, talented freshman Charles Greenhill, and booster Glenn Jones, to attend the Lawrenceburg (Tn.) Quarterback Club Awards Banquet. In the keynote speech Rex had planned to tell his young audience how to meet the challenges of life head-on and the importance of love in a winning record.

Rex never delivered his message. Early that evening his plane went down. All four men were killed.

Rex was one of God's more noble creations. I know. He was my best friend. He was my husband. With a shock of red hair, freckles, and upside-down grin, he was one of those rare individuals you never forget — a disarming Huck Finn-Tom Sawyer all rolled into one.

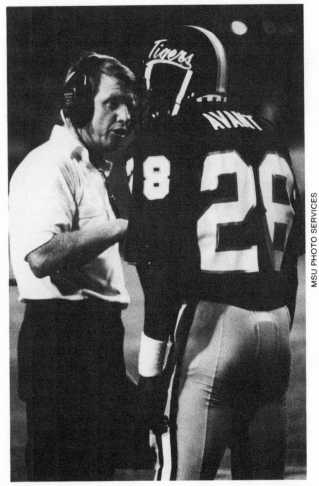

MSU PHOTO SERVICES

INTRODUCTION

(continued)

Rex believed that being a coach was an honor and shaping young lives, a responsibility. His job was to make the most of human potential...from the sports arena to the business world. To do that, he stressed the value of an education and taught mental toughness. He demonstrated the importance of hard work, discipline, laughter, and most of all, love. He demanded much from his players, but he gave back more.

Because of his death at 41, Rex didn't reach all the people he would have with his positive philosophy. It is my hope that this book will start where he left off.

Rex often said, "I believe things happen for a purpose...and according to their own time."

— Wallene Dockery

My grateful appreciation to everyone who helped give birth to this book...who were truly the wind beneath my wings.

PHILOSOPHY

THOMAS BUSLER, THE COMMERCIAL APPEAL

LEADERSHIP

In every field of human endeavor, he that is first
must perpetually live in the white light of publicity.
Whether the leadership be vested in a man or in a
manufactured product, emulation and envy are ever
at work. In art, in literature, in music, in industry,
the reward and the punishment are always the same.
The reward is widespread recognition; the
punishment, fierce denial and detraction. When
a man's work becomes a standard for the whole
world, it also becomes a target for the shafts of the
envious few. If his work be merely mediocre, he will
be left severely alone. If he achieves a masterpiece,
it will set a million tongues a-wagging. Jealousy
does not protrude its forked tongue at the artist who
produces a commonplace painting. Whatsoever
you write or paint or play or sing or build, no one
will strive to surpass or to slander you, unless your
work be stamped with the seal of genius. The leader
is assailed because he is a leader, and the effort to
equal him is merely added proof of that leadership.
If the leader truly leads, he remains — the leader.
Master-poet, master-painter, master-workman,
each in his turn is assailed, and each holds his laurels
through the ages. That which is good or great makes
itself known, no matter how loud the clamor of
denial. That which deserves to live — lives.

— Theodore F. MacManus

NANCY CARLILE

THE OYSTER AND THE EAGLE

When God made the oyster, He guaranteed him
absolute economic and social security. He built the
oyster a house — a shell — to protect him from his
enemies. When hungry, the oyster simply opens his
shell, and food rushes in. He has no worries. He
does not fight anyone. He does not go anywhere.

When God made the eagle, He gave him the sky as his
domain. The eagle then nested on the highest crag.
Storms threaten every day. For food, he flies through
miles of rain, snow, sleet, and wind. He screams his
defiance at the elements. He goes about his own
business, building his own life. When aroused, he's a
vicious foe to his enemies.

The eagle, not the oyster, is the symbol of America.

— Author Unknown

MSU PHOTO SERVICES

18

The courage we desire and prize is not the courage to die decently, but to live manfully.

—Thomas Carlyle

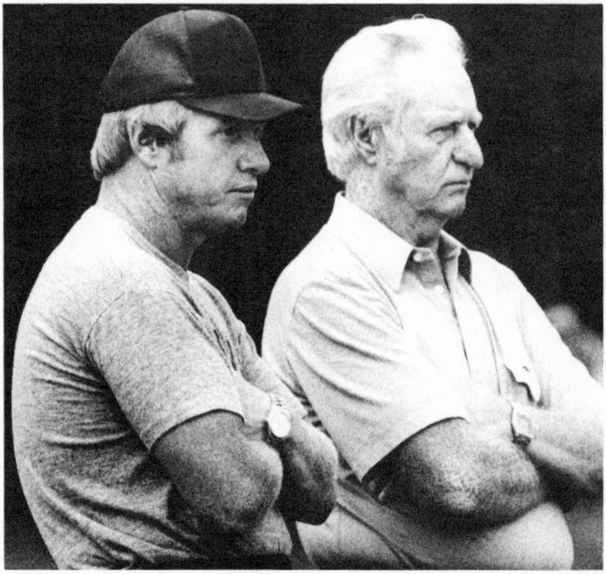

LARRY COYNE, MEMPHIS PRESS-SCIMITAR

IT'S ALL IN THE STATE OF MIND

If you think you are beaten, you are;
If you think you dare not, you don't;
If you like to win but you think you can't,
It's almost a cinch you won't.

If you think you'll lose, you're lost!
For out in the world we find
Success begins with a fellow's will.
It's all in the state of mind.

If you think you're outclassed, you are;
You've got to think high to rise;
You've got to be sure of yourself before
You can ever win the prize.

Life's battles don't always go
To the stronger or faster man,
But sooner or later the man who wins
Is the fellow who thinks he can!

—Walter D. Wintle

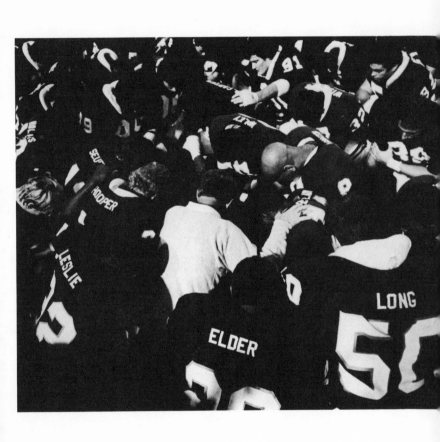

"And we know that all things work together for good to them that love God, to them who are called according to His purpose."

—Romans 8:28

CONSISTENCY

Consistency is the truest measure of performance. Almost anyone can have a great day or even a good year, but true success is the ability to perform day in and day out, year after year, under all kinds of conditions. Inconsistency may win some of the time. Consistency will win most of the time.

Consistency requires concentration, determination and repetition. To be at your best all the time, you must:

1. TAKE NOTHING FOR GRANTED. If you aren't up every day, something or someone will knock you down.
2. TAKE PRIDE IN WHAT YOU KNOW. The things you do well are the things you enjoy doing.
3. TAKE SETBACKS IN STRIDE. Don't brood over reverses; learn from them.
4. TAKE CALCULATED CHANCES. To win something, you must risk something.
5. TAKE WORK HOME. To get ahead, plan ahead.
6. TAKE THE EXTRA LAP. Condition yourself for the long run. The tested can always take it.
7. DON'T TAKE "NO" FOR AN ANSWER. You can do what you believe you can.

CELEBRATE AFTER VICTORY!

— 1983 MSU Playbook

INSPIRATION

LARRY COYNE, MEMPHIS PRESS-SCIMITAR

Keep your long range goals in perspective. Don't worry about the battles. Worry about the war.

You may fail many times, but if you keep on trying, success may be just around the corner.

32

If you would get up every morning, smile until 10:00 a.m., and believe good things are going to happen, you'll be surprised how well your day will go.

You are going to meet both success and failure, but neither one is final. Therefore, be persistent at all times.

Hard work is the most important ingredient of success.

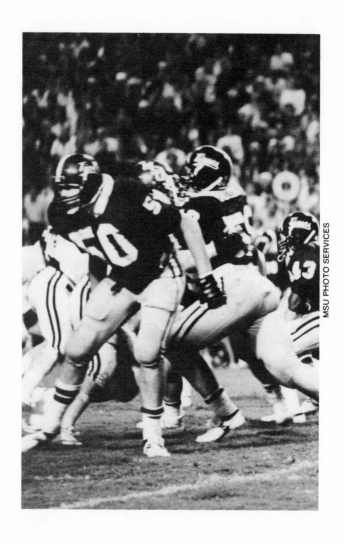

MSU PHOTO SERVICES

A great lesson in human nature is to learn to fight back when things look bad.

Don't confuse effort with results.

Anybody can be average. What do you wish to be?

Being willing to pay the price means persistent self-discipline.

It's all right to fall down as long as you get back up.

Enthusiasm is caught, not taught.

There are three types of players:

> Those who make things happen.
> Those who watch things happen.
> Those who wonder what happened.

TEXAS TECH SPORTS INFORMATION

A player learns from both winning and losing.

Successful players don't rely on talent. They rely on
hard work.

Any man's finest hour is when he lies totally exhausted
on the field of battle...victorious.

— Vince Lombardi

COACHING

RESPECT

1. Respect is an extension of a positive, optimistic attitude.
2. Respect begins with a person having respect for himself.
3. Respect for team members breeds togetherness.
4. Respect has no ethnic, racial or social barriers.
5. A team with respect for one another, wins together.
6. Respect is a two-way street between players and coaches.
7. Make no mistake — football is a team game.
8. Signs of disrespect have negative influences on a team.
9. Successful teams are a family of ONE.
10. Rule of thumb: No one embarrasses anybody in front of his peers or in public.
11. One formula for building respect is developed through an attitude of:
    * PLP = players love players.
    * CLP = coaches love players.
    * PLC = players love coaches.
    * CLC = coaches love coaches.
12. Respect must be earned, not assumed or demanded.

— 1983 MSU Playbook

62

MENTAL ATTITUDE

To win, you must be willing to pay the price. There are no short cuts or magic carpets to championships.

"The heights which great men gained and kept
Were not attained by sudden flight.
But while their companions slept,
Were toiling upward in the night."

—Henry Wadsworth Longfellow

To become champions, you must have desire. Championships do not just happen. They come from within.

It takes hard work to be good.
If we are not good, we have no one to blame but ourselves.

To win, you must believe you can.
When the going gets tough,
The tough get going.

Pride is the basic element in winning.
Teams with pride are the last to surrender.

The difference between winners and losers:
Losers make promises.
Winners make commitments.

—1983 MSU Playbook

"I'll never be content with anything less than being a head coach in a college somewhere. You can't ask a boy to be the best when you're not willing to try it yourself when you get the opportunity."

—Rex Dockery
Chattanooga News-Free Press
August 31, 1973

Dockery, however, does not think the importance of recruiting should be downplayed — as much for the athlete's sake as anyone's.

"It's kind of like being married to somebody for four years," he chuckled.

"You better know them pretty good before you make up your mind."

—Corpus Christi Times
February 7, 1979

FRANKEE RAINS

68

IT COULDN'T BE DONE

Somebody said that it couldn't be done
But he, with a chuckle, replied,

"That maybe it couldn't," but he would be one
Who wouldn't say so til he tried.

So he buckled right in with a trace of a grin
On his face. If he worried, he hid it.

He started to sing as he tackled the thing
That couldn't be done, and he did it!

—Edgar A. Guest

Men stumble over molehills, not mountains.

Look on a problem as an opportunity.

FOOTBALL

TEXAS TECH SPORTS INFORMATION

LAWS OF SUCCESS

Do you want something?...Will you pay
the price?

The great crippler...Fear.

The greatest mistake...Giving up.

The most satisfying experience...
Doing your duty first.

The best action...Keep the mind clear
and judgment good.

The greatest blessing...Good health.

The biggest fool...The man who lies to himself.

The most certain thing in life...Change.

The most potent force...Positive thinking.

The best play...Successful teamwork.

The most expensive indulgence...Hate.

The greatest loss...Loss of self-confidence.

The greatest need...Common sense.

—1983 MSU Playbook

Through intensity and concentration, a player can perform better than his God-given talent would normally allow.

Many times the greatest challenge is not getting to the top, but staying there.

HUMOR

Dockery had some adventures as the Texas Tech coach. His first game was at Southern Cal. The team went to the Los Angeles Coliseum on Friday for a workout. Rex followed the players through the gate. An old man, perhaps a watchman, gave the rookie coach a lift: "Mister, is that all you brought?"

Southern Cal won in the closing two minutes.

—Marvin West
The Knoxville News-Sentinel
December 18, 1980

Rex told the Reader's Digest story of two frogs who accidentally jumped into a bucket of cream:

"I may as well give up," said one frog. "We're goners."

"Keep on paddling," said the other. "We'll get out of this mess somehow."

"No use," the first frog said. "It's too thick to swim, too thin to jump, and too slippery to crawl. We're bound to die sometime, so it may as well be now." He promptly sank to the bottom of the bucket and drowned.

But the second frog just kept on paddling. By morning, he was perched on a mass of butter, which he had churned all by himself.

"You see," Rex would say. "The second frog knew something mighty important; if you work at it long enough, you're bound to come out a winner!"

—Wallene Dockery

BARNEY SELLERS, THE COMMERCIAL APPEAL

Rex also spun the yarn of the wealthy Texan who gave a party and promised his beautiful daughter, three oil wells, and half of his money to any eligible man with the courage and skill to swim across his alligator-filled swimming pool.

Immediately, someone splashed in and swam like mad to the other side.

The wealthy Texan ran over to the young man and congratulated him on his courage. He then asked the young man which prize he would like first.

The young man responded, "I'd like the name of the son-of-a-gun who pushed me into the pool."

—George Lapides
Memphis Press-Scimiter
February 27, 1981

90

Dockery recalled his first season (1973) as Vanderbilt's offensive line coach. He had lost his two top centers in the first two games and had to go into the Alabama game with a third-stringer who had never played a down.

"We had just lost to Mississippi State 58-21 the same day that Alabama was beating California 77-0," he said. "But I told this boy that we had a chance to beat Alabama if he played good.

"They scored on their first two possessions to go ahead 14-0. The next time my center came off the field, he said, 'Coach, take me out. They're beating the hell out of me.' I said, 'Frank, you've got to have a positive attitude.' And he said, 'Okay, I'm positive they're beating the hell out of me'!"

> — Ben Byrd
> Knoxville Journal
> October 16, 1982

REMEMBERING

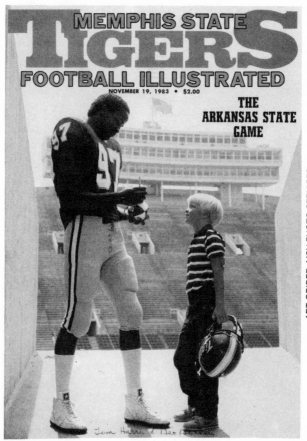

MEMPHIS STATE TIGERS

FOOTBALL ILLUSTRATED

NOVEMBER 19, 1983 • $2.00

THE
ARKANSAS STATE
GAME

ART GRIDER, MSU PHOTO SERVICES

Throughout Dee Dockery's short eight years with his father, the two shared a special bond. I don't know how they could have loved each other any more.

When Rex died, my first thoughts were that Dee would feel abandoned, deserted, and angry. He didn't. Instead, he decided that his father was just as real as ever...and that he loved us as always, even though he lived somewhere else. And despite the traumas we have gone through since, Dee's faith has never wavered.

I got an inkling of Dee's thoughts the first morning following Rex's death. "Mother," he told me, "Dad's started the HFL."

"What?" I was so numb from the shock and lack of sleep that I found it hard to concentrate.

"The HFL," he said. "You know...the Heaven Football League. And he even has Bear Bryant to help him."

—Wallene Dockery

17 REBELS : 9:19 : TIGERS 34
3DOWN 9TO GO BALL ON 4 QTR4

FROM THE FAMILY . . .

Morals and the difference between right and wrong —
that is what my father succeeded in teaching me and
many other young people whose lives he touched.
Although he had strict rules for us to follow, we
learned even more from the way he lived. Rex Dockery
was our example.

My father did not know the word "prejudice". White,
black, or whatever, he related to you as a person, not
according to your ethnic group.

He also taught me the real meaning of family. Even
though he had to work long hours and spend
much time traveling, he was a devoted family man. We
knew that the minute he was finished with work,
he'd be heading home to be with us.

In the last six months, our relationship had changed.
Rex became not only my father, but also my best
friend. Our friendship was something special.
Although his death was the worst thing that has ever
happened to me, I am just thankful to have had twelve
and a half years with him...especially those last six
months.

—Trey Dockery

FROM THE FAMILY . . .

Rex taught us that good things happen if we believe in ourselves.

—John Mull, nephew

Rex never did anything halfway. Our family had a party for his 25th birthday, and Mom baked a coconut cake. After he made a wish, he blew so hard, he blew the icing, coconut, and candles right off the cake.

—Pam Dockery Mull, sister

When Rex entered a room, it was as if someone opened the curtains and let the sunshine in.

—Jan Link, cousin

FROM HIS PLAYERS . . .

Coach Dockery said he didn't want the best 11 players on the field. He wanted the 11 who played best together. The players became like brothers. His death shocked us, but God has a perfect plan. We were blessed to have known him in this lifetime. He loved us...and we loved him.

—Clyde Avant
MSU football 1979-83

FROM HIS PLAYERS . . .

He taught us that "Players Love Players, Coaches
Love Players, Players Love Coaches, Coaches
Love Coaches." We all knew what it meant, and we
lived it.

—Percy Nabors
MSU Team Captain 1983

"We're going to roll up our sleeves," Coach said. "I'll
put my back to yours, and you put yours to mine.
I'm going to believe in you, and you believe in me.
Together, we will get the job done."

—Jim Kutchback
MSU football 1983-84

I decided to get married my senior year during the
days off before bowl practice. I didn't have much
money for a honeymoon. I called Rex, who had been
my coach at UT the previous year before moving to
Georgia Tech, and he found us a motel.
When we got there, I dropped by to thank him. We
started talking football, and I forgot about the
time. I stayed five hours. My wife hasn't forgiven me to
this day.

—Bill Emendorfer
Tennessee football 1969-72

FROM THE COACHES AND STAFF...

When Rex was at Texas Tech, he constantly bugged me to join him. I'd tell him, "That's too far, Rex. I'm just a Tennessee redneck."

Rex would go on about how great Texas Tech was. That was Rex. Wherever he was, that was the greatest place on earth.

—Ken Hudgens
Vanderbilt Asst. Athletic Director

Rex didn't fake anything. If he hurt, it showed. If he was happy, he laughed — out loud and better than anyone.

—John Cropp
Vanderbilt Asst. Coach

Rex challenged us to live up to the responsibility that came with the title "coach".

—Chip Wisdom
Georgia Tech Asst. Coach

I remember Rex's great sense of humor. In a world sometimes dull and dark, he brought fun and light. His leftover laughter is a gift I will always cherish.

Steve Sloan
Head Football Coach
Duke University

FROM THE COACHES AND STAFF . . .

I told Coach Dockery that in my 30 years with
MSU, this was the closest and finest group of athletes
with whom I had ever worked. I know Rex was
responsible for their love for each other and their
desire to win.

—Dr. Clifton Woolley
MSU Team Physician

Rex was a tremendous person from every stand-
point. Not only was he an outstanding coach, he had
sincere concern for people.

—John Majors
Tennessee Head Coach

One Sunday after a disappointing game, a
Memphis paper blasted Coach Dockery. When he
arrived at the office the next day, there were dark
circles under his eyes and frustration written all over
his face.

"Well, Debbie," he said, trying to smile, "the sun
came up this morning just like it always does,
didn't it?"

—Deborah Foster
Rex Dockery's secretary

FROM THE COACHES AND STAFF . . .

Once before a staff meeting, Coach Dockery was reading a news story about the war in Lebanon. "We're worried about signing football players, while people in Beirut are dying," he said. "Let's keep things in perspective. Compared to those people, we don't have a problem in the world."

—Keith Hackett
MSU Asst. Coach

In three short years Rex united a community and built a fence around Memphis so big that area players wanted nothing more than to stay home and become a Tiger.

—Rocky Felker
Alabama Asst. Coach

Rex reminded me of the farmer who dangled a carrot in front of his donkey to get him to pull the cart. Rex convinced his players that they could reach the carrot, the trip wouldn't be too long, and the load wouldn't be too heavy.

—Vic Wallace
Wm. Jewell Head Coach

Rex was one of my favorite people. You can bet he and Coach (Bear) Bryant have organized the 11 best players in heaven and are getting ready for fall.

—Bill Battle
Former Tennessee Head Coach

FROM THE COACHES AND STAFF . . .

Once Rex told me to blow the whistle to start practice. I blew, but without enough enthusiasm to suit him.

"Blow the whistle like you mean it, Coach," he yelled. I've never forgotten. It affects me everytime I pick up a whistle. That was the way Rex wanted you to do everything — like you really meant it.

—Wayne Stiles
Ole Miss Asst. Coach

FROM HIS FRIENDS . . .

Rex shared his life to make others better athletes, better Christians, and better people.

—Joe Rodgers
Cleveland, Tn.

During the dedication of the Liberty Bowl Stadium/ Rex Dockery Field, I realized I couldn't remember who had won the national championship in years past and that those ten scholarships and the field in Rex's honor would have more impact than any championship ever could.

—Jim Walker
Oklahoma City, Okla.

He gave our city and school a touch of success and class. He paved the way.

—George Barham
Memphis, Tn.

FROM HIS FRIENDS . . .

The length of our stay here is not nearly as important as the quality of what we do. I don't know anyone who used his time on earth to better advantage than Rex Dockery.

—Judge Lewis Conner, Jr.
Tennessee Court of Appeals

The outpouring of love and respect for Rex was unprecedented in my memory and reflects our entire city's recognition of his Christian leadership and his strong impact on the lives of the young people he touched.

—William Morris
Shelby County Mayor

Rex Dockery proved that winning does not have to be by intimidation, that success does not have to be built on hype, that how you play the game still counts.

—W. Gregg Jones
Memphis, Tn.

I am proud that he called me his friend.

—John Elkington
Memphis, Tn.

FROM HIS FRIENDS . . .

Rex operated at a pace and level of enthusiasm I
didn't think possible for an entire football team,
much less one person.

—Avron Fogelman
Owner, Kansas City Royals
Memphis, Tn.

I moved to Memphis in 1981 to organize a
professional indoor soccer team. Very quickly I
realized that Rex and I both had uphill battles. Yet,
it wasn't until a Special Olympics golf event that
we finally had the chance to meet.

That day Rex and I joined the others in reciting the
oath: "Let me win; but if I cannot win, let me be
brave in the attempt."

When we finished, a Special Athlete, not realizing
the poor prognosis for the Tigers, asked, "Coach,
are you gonna be number one?" Rex smiled.
"We will win, but if we cannot win, we will be brave
in the attempt."

—Kyle Rote, Jr.
Memphis, Tn.

FROM HIS FRIENDS . . .

When Rex joined MSU in 1981, I was assigned to prepare a football start-of-a-new-era poster. My first "rough" emphasized a head-and-shoulders shot of Rex with highlights of MSU and Memphis in the background.

As soon as Rex saw my proposal, he called. "I want our new A.D. to be in the poster and all of my assistant coaches, too." He was diplomatic, but emphatic.

I hesitated. Twelve additional portraits meant hours of extra work, but Rex insisted it would help the football program. He was so persuasive, I agreed. I realized then Rex would never have "I" trouble.

—Ted Watts
Sports Artist

FROM THE PRESS . . .

Coach Dockery pulled the campus and community together as nobody else had. He never blamed players for bad plays. If the team lost on Saturday, he told the press that he would have to do a better job of teaching for the next game. This was unique in a world when many coaches have giant-sized egos.

—Mark Hayden
MSU Daily Helmsman

FROM THE PRESS . . .

(Once) I questioned Rex about his decision to accept the Memphis State job, and he gave me a good scolding. "I think it can be one of the best coaching situations in the South," he said. "We can and will get this thing turned around. You just watch."

I didn't talk to Rex much during the next two years. I knew MSU was struggling. In fact, I was scared for Dockery and the program.

Rex entered the 1983 season with even more fire and determination. MSU won the opener, but dropped the next three.

Then, suddenly, two super recruiting years began to pay off. The Tigers started to win, and the fans went crazy. The Dockery Era was about to take over.

Those precious moments in the dressing room after a big win over Vandy won't be forgotten. Rex was standing there with that same big grin. He looked so satisfied. "I told you we could do it," he beamed. "Tell the rest of the boys (at your paper), we still play football in West Tennessee."

—George Starr
Chattanooga News-Free Press

Honor, integrity, and character were descriptions that rested easily on his shoulders.

—Editorial
The Cleveland (Tn.) Daily Banner

FROM THE PRESS . . .

Rex was about to turn a "have-not" into a "have". He was in the process of beating the odds.

—George Lapides
Memphis Press-Scimitar

Rex loved to visit his hometown of Cleveland (Tn.) as often as possible. "It recharges the old batteries," he would grin. "You should never, ever forget where you came from."

—Mike Fleming
The Commercial Appeal

What many of us will remember forever about Rex Dockery was his unsinkable spirit and his unquenchable belief that better things were always within the grasp of those willing to work hard enough to attain them.

—Al Dunning
The Commercial Appeal

With his shock of red hair and infectious, bubbling personality, knowing him was like having Huckleberry Finn as a best friend.

—Pat Embry
Nashville Banner

EPILOGUE

Thomas Forest once said:
    "A man's ambition should be high,
    Not scratched in the dirt,
    But carved in the sky."

Those of you who knew and loved Rex Dockery
knew him as a man with a dream...not for himself,
but for his home, Memphis, and for his university,
Memphis State.

You see, he loved his city, and he loved his school.
Together he felt the two could do amazing things.

Today, Rex's home is somewhere else...a place
we're not yet privileged to visit. But if he were here
tonight, I know he would be deeply moved and
touched by the honor Memphis has bestowed on
him.

My only wish is that in the future when we think of the
Liberty Bowl Memorial Stadium/Rex Dockery Field,
we will remember Rex's vision of greatness for
Memphis and for Memphis State...and we will be
reminded that his dream can only become reality by all
of us working together.

                    Thank you and God bless you.
                    —Wallene Dockery

        May 5, 1984: From the dedication of the Liberty
        Bowl Memorial Stadium/Rex Dockery Field.

CHRONOLOGY

1942   Feb. 7, born in Cleveland, Tn., to
            John ("Red") and Jeannette Dockery.

1959   Selected All State as guard; leads
            Bradley Central High to 11-0 season;
            selected team co-captain.

1960-64   Played football at Tennessee under
            head coaches Bowden Wyatt and Jim
            McDonald.

1964-65   Tennessee graduate assistant coach
            under Doug Dickey.

1966-67   Head coach, Harriman (Tn.) High
            School.

1968-69   Head coach, Morristown East (Tn.)
            High School. Twice Big 7 Conference
            Coach of the Year, wins State AAA
            Championship. Named #3 team in
            nation.

1970-71   Tennessee assistant coach under
            Bill Battle.

            July 10, marries Wallene Threadgill
            Cates.

1972   Georgia Tech assistant coach under
            Bill Fulcher.

1973-74   Vanderbilt offensive coordinator under
           Steve Sloan.
           Adopts Trey, Wallene's son.

1975   March 22, son, John Dee born.
           Coaches in Kodak All-American Game.

1975-77   Offensive coordinator at Texas Tech
           under Steve Sloan.

1978-80   Head football coach at Texas Tech.

1978   Named Southwestern Conference Coach
           of the Year by AP, UPI, and state
           newspapers; Senior College Coach of
           the Year; American Football Coaches
           District VII Coach of the Year.

1980-83   Head football coach at Memphis State
           University.

1983   Nov. 28, NCAA names MSU second
           most improved team in the nation, and
           number one in increased attendance.
           Dec. 5, Rex Dockery chosen Metro
           Conference Coach of the Year.
           Dec. 12, killed in plane crash with
           Chris Faros, Charles Greenhill, and
           Glenn Jones near Lawrenceburg, Tn.

1984   May 5, dedication of Liberty Bowl
           Memorial Stadium/Rex Dockery Field
           in Memphis, Tn.

PHOTOGRAPHS

These photographs are of the following individuals: